THE STORY OF THE BROOKLYN NETS

Buck Williams

Joe Harris

A HISTORY OF HOOPS

THE STORY OF THE

BROOKLYN
NETS

JIM WHITING

Derrick Coleman

CREATIVE SPORTS

CREATIVE EDUCATION / CREATIVE PAPERBACKS

Published by Creative Education and Creative Paperbacks
P.O. Box 227, Mankato, Minnesota 56002
Creative Education and Creative Paperbacks are imprints of
The Creative Company
www.thecreativecompany.us

Design and production by Blue Design (www.bluedes.com)
Art direction by Rita Marshall
Production layout by Rachel Klimpel and Ciara Beitlich

Photographs by Access Hollywood Online (elitesports1010), AP Images (Ross
Franklin, John Minchillo, Kevin Reece, Corey Sipkin), Ebay (illini37), Getty
(Nic Antaya, Nathaniel S. Butler, Lou Capozzola, Jonathan Daniel, Ned
Dishman, Focus On Sport, Jesse D. Garrabrant, Dwight Howard, Fernando
Medina, Manny Millan, Ronald C. Modra/Sports Imagery, New York Daily
News Archive, Michael Reaves, Sarah Stier), Shutterstock (Brocreative,
Valentin Valkov), StickPNG (Brooklyn Nets)

Library of Congress Cataloging-in-Publication Data
Names: Whiting, Jim, 1943- author.
Title: The story of the Brooklyn Nets / by Jim Whiting.
Description: Mankato, Minnesota : Creative Education | Creative
  Paperbacks, [2023] | Series: Creative Sports: A History of Hoops | Includes
  index. | Audience: Ages 8-12 years | Audience: Grades 4-6 | Summary:
  "Middle grade basketball fans are introduced to the extraordinary history
  of NBA's Brooklyn Nets with a photo-laden narrative of their greatest
  successes and losses"-- Provided by publisher.
Identifiers: LCCN 2022007484 (print) | LCCN 2022007485 (ebook) | ISBN
  9781640266193 (Library Binding) | ISBN 9781682771754 (Paperback) | ISBN
  9781640007604 (eBook)
Subjects: LCSH: Brooklyn Nets (Basketball team)--History--Juvenile
  literature.
Classification: LCC GV885.52.B76 W557 2023 (print) | LCC GV885.52.B76
  (ebook) | DDC 796.323/640974723--dc23/eng/20220604
LC record available at https://lccn.loc.gov/2022007484
LC ebook record available at https://lccn.loc.gov/2022007485

Seth Curry

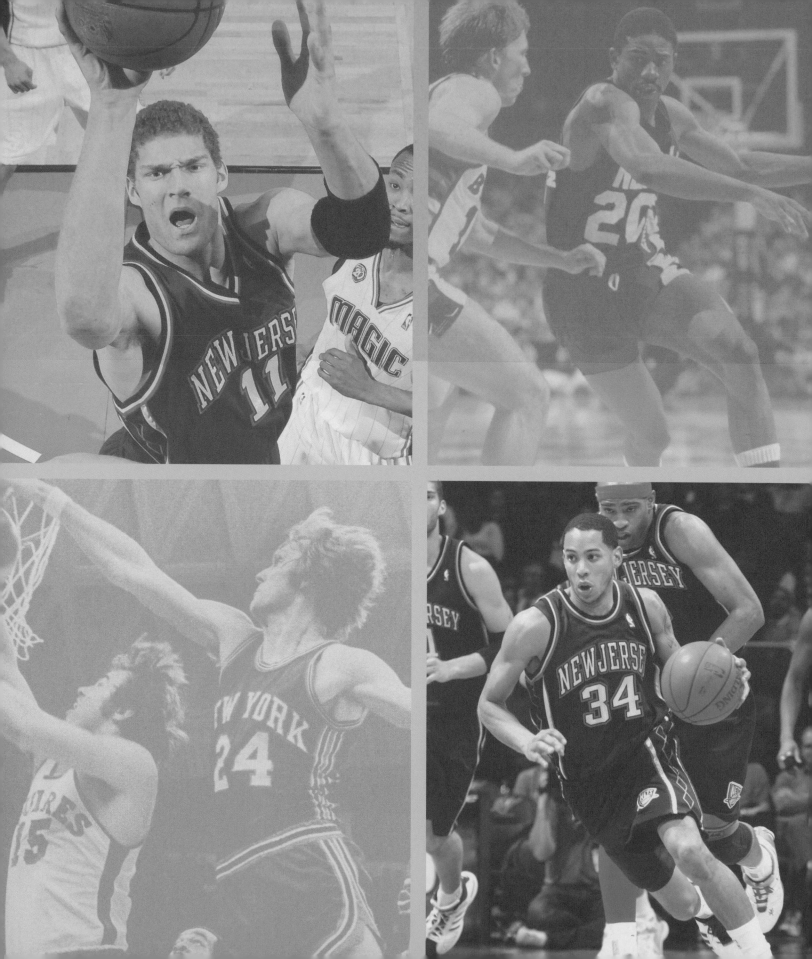

CONTENTS

LEGENDS OF THE HARDWOOD

Kevin Durant

A MATTER OF INCHES

t was the final moments of Game 7 of the Eastern Conference semifinals in 2021. The Milwaukee Bucks clung to a 109–107 lead. Brooklyn Nets superstar Kevin Durant took a long inbound pass by the scorer's table. He dribbled toward the top of the key. He spun to his left, spun again. With one second remaining, he launched a long fallaway jump shot at the three-point line. Nothing but net! Nets win! Jubilant Nets players poured onto the court. But wait. The play had to be reviewed. Replays showed that Durant's toes were clearly touching the three-point line. That meant the shot counted for two points, not three. The score became 109–109. That forced the game into overtime. The Bucks outscored the Nets, 6–2 in the extra session. Brooklyn's season was over.

The Nets story began in 1967. The new American Basketball Association (ABA) wanted a team in New York City but there wasn't a suitable arena. In desperation, owner Arthur Brown settled on Teaneck Armory just across the Hudson River from New York City. Brown named his team the New Jersey Americans. In their first season, they finished in a tie for the fourth and final playoff berth against the Kentucky Colonels. League officials scheduled a one-game playoff.

LEGENDS
OF THE HARDWOOD

RICK BARRY
SMALL FORWARD
HEIGHT: 6-FOOT-7
NETS SEASONS: 1970–72

THE DIFFERENCE MAKER

Rick Barry led the NBA in scoring in 1966–67 at nearly 36 points a game with the San Francisco Warriors. It was just his second year in the league. Then the Oakland Oaks of the rival ABA offered him a huge contract. The Warriors took him to court. A judge ruled that he had to sit out a year. After one-year stints with two ABA teams, Barry's rights were sold to the Nets prior to the 1970–71 season. The following season, he played a key role as the team advanced to the ABA Finals against Indiana. The Pacers won though, 4 games to 2. Barry was second in the ABA in scoring in 1971–72 at over 31 points a game. Following the season, a judge ruled he had to return to the NBA and the Warriors. Barry was a 12-time All-Star across both leagues and is in the Basketball Hall of Fame.

Rick Barry

A circus had already booked Teaneck Armory. The team settled for Long Island's Commack Arena instead. The short notice for preparation caused a lot of sloppiness. The 3-point line was crooked. One basket was higher than the other. The floor was slick from a hockey game the night before. Some floorboards were loose. Kentucky refused to play there. ABA commissioner George Mikan forced the Americans to forfeit.

The team moved to Long Island the following year. It became the New York Nets, to rhyme with two other local teams: Jets of the American Football League and Mets of Major League Baseball.

The team played like its name was "Not Yets." Its record was a dismal 17–61. Only about 1,000 people showed up for each home game. Brown sold the team. New owner Roy Boe moved the Nets to a better arena. The team improved to 39–45. The Nets made the playoffs. They lost in the first round. The team signed Rick Barry for the 1970–71 season. He was a superstar from the rival league, the National Basketball Association (NBA). "Rick was a scoring machine," said Dan Issel, who often played against him. "I once heard him say that he expected to score 30 points a night. He had it all figured out: he'd take 20 shots, make 12, and then he'd get to the foul line 6 or 8 times to pick up the rest."

His plan worked. Barry averaged 29.4 points per game that season. With a 40–44 record, the Nets squeezed into the playoffs. Again they lost in the first round. Barry did even better the next year, averaging 31.5 points per game. The Nets achieved their first winning record, 44–40. They shocked the basketball world by advancing to the ABA Finals. But they could not keep up with the tough Indiana Pacers. The Nets lost, 4 games to 2.

THE DOCTOR IS IN

n 1972, the term "full-court press" soon took on a different meaning. When Barry left the NBA to join the ABA, he still had one more year in his contract. A judge ruled in court that Barry had to return to the NBA league. Without him, the Nets struggled to a 30–54 mark in the 1972–73 season. The cash-strapped Virginia Squires sold budding star Julius Erving to the Nets. "Dr. J" soon became famous for the way he "operated" on the court. The 6-foot-7 small forward moved with astonishing speed and grace. His spectacular dunks filled highlight films.

Before Erving, almost all dunks came from big men. They stood beneath the basket. Then they jumped straight up and hurled the ball into the hoop. Erving was different. He started off 15 feet from the basket or even further. He would soar high into the air and then dunk. He originated the term "slam dunk." Massive center Artis Gilmore often faced him. "We all became entangled in what he was going to do," he said. "He was the ooh and aah guy. His dunks were adventures. His dunks made a difference."

That difference wasn't just the two points each dunk added to his team's score. The high-flying hoop fest fired up the home crowd. During Dr. J's first year as a Net, the home crowd had plenty to cheer about. The team racked up 55 wins, 25 more than the previous season. The Nets roared through the playoffs. They lost just two games in three different series. The Nets crushed the Utah Stars in the Finals. They won their first ABA championship! Erving won the league's Most Valuable Player (MVP) award. Fans looked forward to another championship the following year. In a stunning upset, the Nets lost, 4 games to 1, to the Spirits of St. Louis in the first round of the playoffs. The Nets had finished 26 games ahead

JULIUS ERVING
SMALL FORWARD
HEIGHT: 6-FOOT-7
NETS SEASONS: 1973–76

WHAT'S IN A NAME?

Julius Erving's "Dr. J" nickname originated in high school. "I had a friend who had a habit of arguing a point and going on to lecture the person he was arguing with, so I called him 'The Professor,'" Erving explained. "After that he started calling me 'The Doctor.' It had something to do with the saying, 'He has more moves than Carter has pills.'" (The Carter Company made medicine.) When Erving joined the Virginia Squires in 1971, a teammate started saying, "There's the doctor digging into his bag again," whenever he dunked the ball. "Dr. Julius" soon became "Dr. J." It is one of the most famous nicknames in NBA history.

BROOKLYN NETS

13

of the Spirits during the regular season. They also won all 11 games between the two teams during the regular season. The Nets wouldn't be denied in 1975–76. They romped to their second title. Dr. J won his third straight league MVP award.

The ABA and NBA merged after the 1976 season. The Nets had to pay a $3 million entrance fee to join the NBA. They also had to pay the New York Knicks another $4.8 million for moving into the Knicks' NBA "territory." In order to afford these two costs, Boe had to take back the raise he had promised Erving. Dr. J. refused to play. The Philadelphia 76ers offered the Nets $3 million for him. "How could anyone do this to us?" asked Nets guard John Williamson. "Our season is over already." Williamson was right. The Nets finished their first NBA season with a 22–60 record. It was the worst in the league. "The merger agreement killed the Nets as an NBA franchise," Boe said years later. "It forced me to destroy the team by selling Erving to pay the bill." The team did have one noteworthy event. In a game in February, they became the first team with a starting lineup of all left-handers.

The New York Nets in the ABA – 1974

LEGENDS
OF THE HARDWOOD

DARRYL DAWKINS
CENTER
HEIGHT: 6-FOOT-11
NETS SEASONS: 1982–87

THUNDER DUNKING

When Dawkins joined the Nets, he already had a reputation for his powerful
slam dunks. His style was so different from Dr. J's graceful glides to the hoop.
Dawkins called himself Dr. Dunkenstein. Pop singer Stevie Wonder gave him
a different (and better-known) nickname: Chocolate Thunder. Dawkins was
also known as a rim-wrecker. In 1979, he dunked so hard the glass in the
backboard shattered. He did it again three weeks later. "The first one was
an accident, but I wanted to see if I could do it again," Dawkins said years
later. "All the fans were hollering, 'You've got to do one for the home crowd,'
so I went ahead and brought it down." After that, the NBA made a new rule
that anyone who broke the backboard would be fined and suspended. Today's
hoops have hinges that allow them to bend without breaking the backboard.

RETURNING TO THEIR ROOTS

Not surprisingly, few fans turned out for the 1976–77 season. Boe moved the Nets back to New Jersey before the 1977–78 season. Small forward Bernard King joined the team. He made the NBA All-Rookie team by scoring 1,909 points in his first season. But he lasted only two seasons. The Nets continued to struggle. Veteran coach Larry Brown took the reins for the 1981–82 season. He sparked the Nets to their first winning record in six years. They finished at 44–38. One key was rugged power forward Buck Williams. He averaged 12 rebounds and 15 points. He was named NBA Rookie of the Year. "Every team should be blessed with a Buck Williams," said Barry. "He's consistent, hardworking, and tough." The Nets did even better the following year. They won 49 games. It was their best record in the NBA. However, Coach Brown had taken a college coaching job in the last month of the season. The team lost four of its final six games. They quickly bowed out of the playoffs.

Team officials surrounded Williams with talent. Micheal Ray Richardson stepped in as point/shooting guard, "dunkmeister" Darryl Dawkins took over at center, and versatile Albert King (Bernard's younger brother) boosted the team's point totals. The Nets advanced to the Eastern Conference semifinals the following season. But they lost to the Bucks. They made the playoffs again the following two seasons. Both times they were bounced in the first round. Injuries and off–court issues plagued the Nets for several years after that. They hit rock bottom in 1989–90. Their 17–65 record was the worst in team history.

In 1991–92, the Nets recorded a 40–42 mark. They returned to the playoffs for the first time in six years. Solid draft choices such as power forward/center Derrick Coleman and point guard Kenny Anderson boosted the team. They lost to Cleveland in the first round. With the help of Croatian shooting guard Dražen Petrović, the Nets enjoyed their first winning mark in seven seasons in 1992–93. But again, the Nets could not make it through the first round. Petrović tragically died in an automobile accident a few weeks later.

Once again, the team went into a tailspin. Between 1994–95 and 2000–01, the Nets had just one winning season and playoff appearance. That came in 1997–98. The Nets faced superstar Michael Jordan and the Chicago Bulls, who easily swept the series. The team collapsed in the lockout-shortened 1998–99 season. They won just 16 games. Two more losing seasons followed.

UP, DOWN, AND UP AGAIN

The Nets had a dramatic turnout in 2001–02. They drafted small forward Richard Jefferson. The team also made one of its best-ever trades. They acquired veteran point/shooting guard Jason Kidd. It paid immediate dividends. The Nets soared to an all-time franchise-best 52–30 mark. "This team has taken on Jason's soul," said TV commentator and former player Danny Ainge. "Some guys show up to play; some guys show up to win. But the way Jason plays, he elevates everyone else's game because they go, 'My gosh, look at how hard he plays, look how confident he is, look at how tough-minded he is.' It's contagious for the rest of them. They see how hard you have to play to win."

Dražen Petrović

The team cruised through the first three rounds of the playoffs. Then they faced the Los Angeles Lakers in their first-ever trip to the NBA Finals. Led by superstars Shaquille O'Neal and Kobe Bryant, the Lakers swept the series. The Nets had to be satisfied with losing three of the games by six points or less.

They proved that it wasn't a fluke the following season. After defeating the Bucks in the first round, the Nets swept both the Boston Celtics and Detroit Pistons for their second straight trip to the Finals. This time they faced the San Antonio Spurs and their future Hall of Fame duo of Tim Duncan and David Robinson. The Spurs won in six games.

Gifted swingman Vince Carter helped the Nets remain near the top of the league the following four seasons. During this period, they advanced to the conference semifinals three times.

Kidd, Carter, and Jefferson left to play elsewhere. The Nets failed to make the playoffs for the following five seasons. The Nets lost their first 18 games in 2009–10. It was the worst start in NBA history. They plummeted to a final 12–70 mark. Midway through 2011–12, the team added All-Star point guard Deron Williams. Unfortunately, injuries kept the team from taking full advantage of him.

Vince Carter

JASON KIDD
POINT GUARD
HEIGHT: 6-FOOT-4
NETS SEASONS:
2001—08 AS PLAYER
2013—14 AS COACH

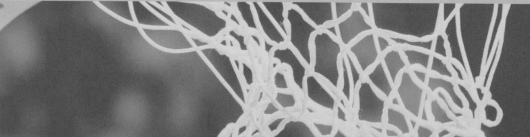

LEADING TO VICTORY

Jason Kidd had a spectacular California high school career. Dozens of major colleges wanted him. He chose nearby California-Berkeley. The not-so-Golden Bears won just 10 games the previous season. Kidd helped remove the tarnish. He led Cal to two NCAA tournament berths. He was an All-American as a sophomore. He entered the draft the following season. Dallas made him the second overall pick. He joined the Nets seven years later. Kidd became the team's on-court leader. They made the playoffs all but one year he played. He rejoined the Nets in 2013–14 as coach. After a slow start, they made the playoffs.

ROBIN LOPEZ
CENTER
HEIGHT: 7-FOOT-0

BROOK LOPEZ
CENTER
HEIGHT: 7-FOOT-0
NETS SEASONS:
2008–2017

Robin & Brook Lopez

TWIN TOWERS

Seven-footers Brook and Robin Lopez are the tallest twins in the NBA. Brook averaged 19 points in 2007–08 as the brothers helped Stanford University to the NCAA Sweet Sixteen. The twins were drafted into the NBA in 2008. Robin was picked up by the Phoenix Suns. Brook was picked 10th overall by the Nets and quickly moved into their starting lineup. He finished with an average of 13 points a game. His 154 blocked shots were fourth in the NBA. He was named to the NBA All-Rookie first team. When he left the Nets seven years later, he was the team's all-time leading scorer. Off the court, the brothers used their basketball experiences to collaborate on a manga called Transition Game in 2021.

NEW START IN NEW YORK

The Nets relocated to Brooklyn before the 2012–13 season. It was the first time the city had a major professional team since baseball's Dodgers moved to Los Angeles following the 1957 season. The Nets got a new arena and new uniforms. They won 49 games. That was more than the total of the two previous seasons in New Jersey. The Nets and Bulls split the first six games of their first-round playoff series. Twenty-one thousand roaring fans packed Barclays Center for Game 7. Brooklyn fell behind by 17 points at halftime. They closed the gap to four points in the third quarter. That was as close as they got. The Nets lost 99–93. Despite the loss, it seemed clear that Brooklyn fans finally had something to cheer.

The following season, Brooklyn acquired two veterans from the Celtics, power forward/center Kevin Garnett and small forward/shooting guard Paul Pierce. "We have achieved a great balance on our roster between veteran stars and young talents," said Nets principal owner Mikhail Prokhorov. "This team will be dazzling to watch and tough to compete against."

After a 10–21 start, the team leapt to a 44–38 regular season record. Brooklyn defeated Toronto in the first round of the playoffs. But they were burned by the Miami Heat in the next round. Pierce moved on as the Nets stumbled in the 2014–15 season. They finished just 38–44. They still made the playoffs again, only to lose in the first round. Garnett and Williams both left the team.

Despite solid play from center Brook Lopez and Croatian small forward Bojan Bogdanović, the Nets' 2015–16 season ended in a disappointing 21 wins. Even more disappointing was a 1–25 mark in January and February of the following season. They finished 20–62. The 2017–18 season wasn't much better. Brooklyn had just 28 wins. They improved to 42–40 the following season but fell to the 76ers in the first round of the playoffs.

The team signed superstar point guard Kyrie Irving before the 2019–20 season. He became the first player in NBA history to notch 50 points in his debut game with a new team. But he underwent season-ending surgery the following January. Even worse, the COVID-19 pandemic forced league officials to suspend play for more than four months. After play resumed, the Nets finished 35–37. It was good enough for the playoffs. Toronto swept them.

Brooklyn had also signed Kevin Durant, even though he had suffered a ruptured Achilles tendon during the previous season and would need more than a year to recover.

The Nets weren't done beefing up their roster. Partway through the 2020–21 season, they traded for Houston shooting guard James Harden. "It's an amazing move for Brooklyn. Obviously, they got better—way better," said Milwaukee's Giannis Antetokounmpo, a two-time MVP. Harden became the first player in NBA history to record a triple-double in his debut with a new team. The team had been barely over .500 when he arrived. They finished strongly even though Durant

Kevin Durant

Kyrie Irving

JAY-Z

B IS FOR BROOKLYN

To make the move to Brooklyn more exciting, the Nets adopted new logos and uniforms. Rapper and businessman JAY-Z designed their new look. He is a Brooklyn native who is married to pop superstar Beyoncé. The logo features a prominent letter B. It is similar to logos the New York subway system used during the 1950s. "Our black-and-white colors speak to Brooklyn's strong traditions and grittiness and convey an uncompromising confidence," said CEO Brett Yormark. "We are thrilled to launch our brand and to introduce the Brooklyn community to its new team. It's an honor to bring major professional sports back to Brooklyn and to become part of the fabric of this great borough."

missed half the season with a variety of injuries. The 48–24 final mark made them the second seed in the Eastern Conference playoffs. They easily brushed aside the Celtics. That set up a memorable series with the Bucks and Durant's oh-so-close jump shot as time expired.

The team had high hopes in 2021–22. They jumped out to a 21–8 record by mid-December but couldn't maintain the pace. By early March they were just 32–33. Durant missed nearly 30 games due to injury. Irving was limited to 29 games because he refused to get the COVID 19 vaccine, which was mandatory for pro athletes playing in New York City. Brooklyn traded Harden midway through the season for Philadelphia star guard Ben Simmons. He was injured at the time and never suited up. The Nets still finished strong with a 44–38 mark. They won a play-in game to make it into the playoffs, but the Celtics swept them in the first round in four close games. The largest margin of victory was just seven points. Irving said his feelings were "disappointment, a little sadness, because we didn't play as well as a team as we wanted to."

Since winning two ABA titles in the mid-1970s, the Nets have come close to basketball glory only a few times. For the city of Brooklyn, the championship sports drought has lasted even longer. Nets fans hope the team will break both droughts soon.

INDEX

Nic Claxton